Celebrations in My World

ELECTION DAY

Lynn Peppas

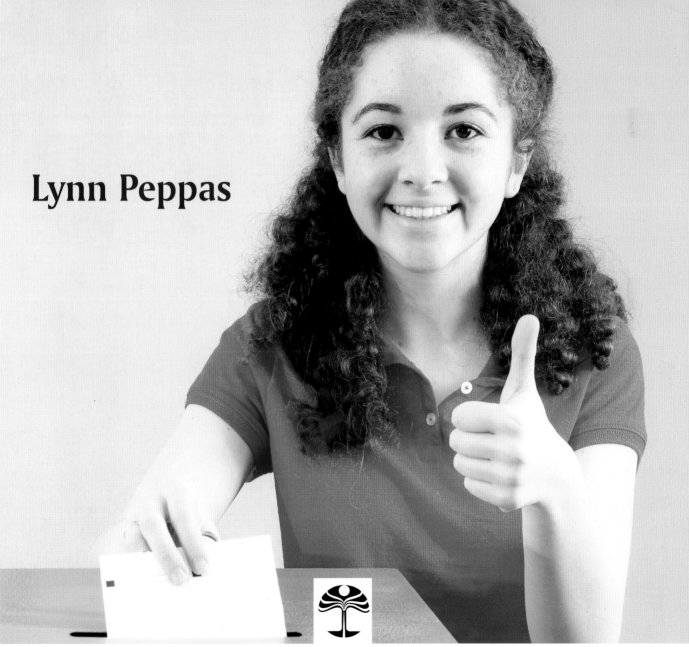

Crabtree Publishing Company
www.crabtreebooks.com

Crabtree Publishing Company

www.crabtreebooks.com

Author: Lynn Peppas
Series and project editor: Susan LaBella
Editor: Adrianna Morganelli
Proofreader: Reagan Miller
Photo research: Crystal Sikkens
Editorial director: Kathy Middleton
Design: Katherine Berti
Suzena Samuel & Ravinder
Chauhan (Q2AMEDIA)
Production coordinator and
Prepress technician: Katherine Berti

Photographs:
Alamy: Jeff Greenberg: pages 10, 23
Associated Press: pages 11, 29
Bettmann/CORBIS: page 8
Dreamstime: pages 4, 6, 16 (calendar), 18, 21
iStockPhoto: page 20
UPPA/Photoshot: page 7
Shutterstock: cover, pages 1, 5, 9, 12, 13, 14, 15,
16 (inset), 17, 19, 22, 24, 25, 26, 27, 28, 30, 31

Library and Archives Canada Cataloguing in Publication

Peppas, Lynn
Election day / Lynn Peppas.

(Celebrations in my world)
Includes index.
Issued also in an electronic format.
ISBN 978-0-7787-4925-7 (bound).--ISBN 978-0-7787-4932-5 (pbk.)

1. Election Day--Juvenile literature. 2. Elections--Juvenile literature.
3. Voting--Juvenile literature. 4. Elections--United States--Juvenile
literature. I. Title. II. Series: Celebrations in my world

JF1001.P46 2010   j324.6'5   C2010-902747-7

Library of Congress Cataloging-in-Publication Data

Peppas, Lynn.
Election day / Lynn Peppas.
p. cm. -- (Celebrations in my world)
Includes index.
ISBN 978-0-7787-4932-5 (pbk. : alk. paper) -- ISBN 978-0-7787-4925-7
(reinforced library binding : alk. paper) -- ISBN 978-1-4271-9442-8
(electronic (pdf))
1. Election Day--Juvenile literature. 2. Elections--United States--Juvenile
literature. 3. Voting--United States--Juvenile literature. 4. Elections--Juvenile
literature. 5. Voting--Juvenile literature. I. Title. II. Series.

JK1978.P47 2010
324.6'50973--dc22

2010016411

Crabtree Publishing Company

www.crabtreebooks.com   1-800-387-7650

Printed in China/082010/AP20100512

Published in Canada
Crabtree Publishing
616 Welland Ave.
St. Catharines, ON
L2M 5V6

Published in the United States
Crabtree Publishing
PMB 59051
350 Fifth Avenue, 59th Floor
New York, New York 10118

Published in the United Kingdom
Crabtree Publishing
Maritime House
Basin Road North, Hove
BN41 1WR

Published in Australia
Crabtree Publishing
386 Mt. Alexander Rd.
Ascot Vale (Melbourne)
VIC 3032

Contents

What Is Election Day?

Election Day is a day when people choose their leaders. Election comes from the word elect. It means to help make a choice or decision.

Every adult gets one vote on Election Day.

VOTE

DID YOU KNOW?

*In most countries a person must be 18 years or older to **vote** in a public election. Those people are called voters.*

Elections in Ukraine fall on different dates.

Different countries around the world have different election days. Some countries have one election day that is always on the same date. In other countries, election days fall on different dates.

What Is Democracy?

Most countries hold elections. They rule by **democracy**. Democracy means that the people from a country help to decide who will make laws. The group of people elected is called a **government**.

● Canadian Prime Minister Stephen Harper is the leader of a democratic government.

DID YOU KNOW?

Democracy comes from a Greek word that means "power to the people."

Thousands of years ago, ancient Greeks were the first people to rule by democracy.

A few countries do not hold elections. A **monarch** or **dictator** rules them. People in these countries do not have a choice about who will rule.

King Mswati III is the ruling monarch of Swaziland.

7

Every Vote Counts

A citizen is someone who belongs to a country. Citizens follow laws and pay **taxes** to their country. The country's government makes sure every citizen has the same **rights**.

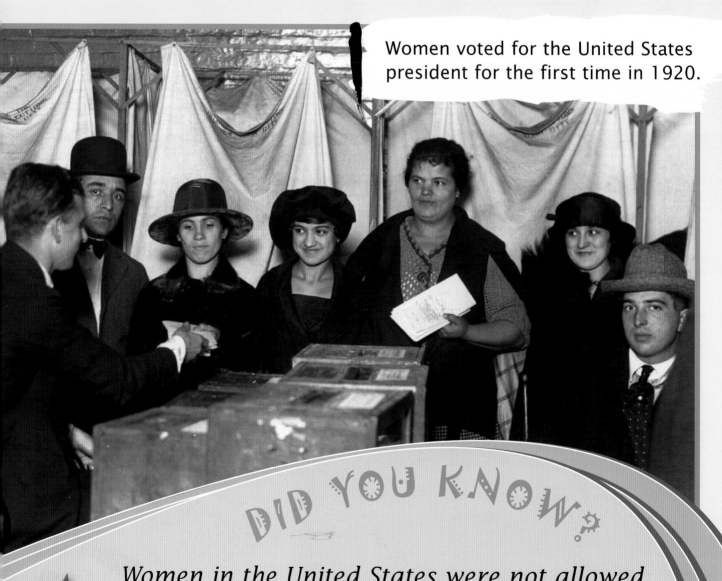

Women voted for the United States president for the first time in 1920.

DID YOU KNOW?

*Women in the United States were not allowed to vote because of their **gender** until 1920.*

Less than 100 years ago, women had to fight for their right to vote.

Citizens in a democracy have the right to vote in an election. This vote helps to decide who should be the leader.

It is important to vote. Voters help decide how a community will be ruled. Elections give people the freedom to choose their leaders.

9

Early and Absentee Voting

Sometimes people are not able to vote on Election Day. They may not be able to vote because of work, vacations, or **religious** or **medical** reasons. Many countries have early voting. This means that citizens can vote before an Election Day.

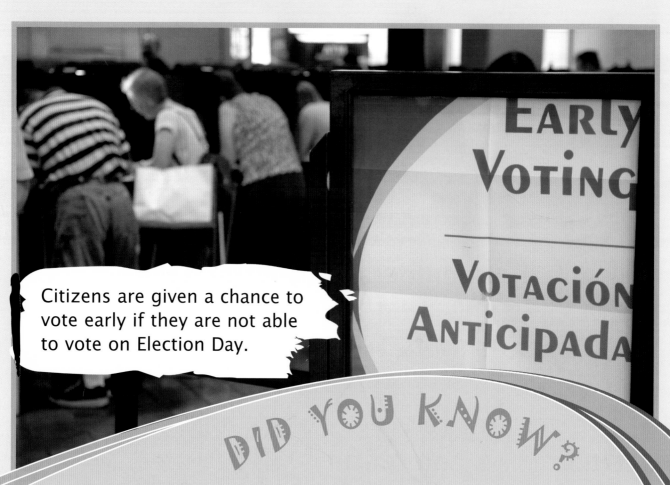

Citizens are given a chance to vote early if they are not able to vote on Election Day.

EARLY VOTING

VOTACIÓN ANTICIPADA

DID YOU KNOW?

Early and absentee voting can be done by mail. Early polling stations are set up for early voters, too.

Soldiers fighting in faraway places still get to vote for their country's leaders.

Absentee voting lets citizens vote when they cannot come to a polling station. Absentee means a person who is away. Some work in other countries such as people in the **military**.

11

Electing Leaders

A leader is a person who makes decisions for a group of people or community. Most times, leaders are elected to their jobs.

- President Barack Obama was elected as leader of the United States.

DID YOU KNOW?

A person who is trying to win an election and become a leader is called a candidate.

The top leader in the United States is called a president. In other countries, a top leader is called a prime minister or chancellor.

Different leaders have different ideas about how to rule a country. People vote for the person that they think will do the best job.

In Germany, the top leader is called a chancellor. This is Chancellor Angela Merkel.

History of Election Day

In the 1800s, most people living in America were farmers. They grew crops for food and money. In the fall, they **harvested** their crops. If an election was in the fall, many were too busy to vote. Farmers that did have time to vote had to travel long distances by horse-drawn vehicles to reach a polling station.

Some citizens had to travel all day in order to vote.

For these reasons, lawmakers decided to hold Election Day in November. In November, harvests were finished and stormy winter weather had not yet started.

Over a hundred years ago, most families in America earned their living by farming.

DID YOU KNOW?

Lawmakers decided to hold Election Day on a Tuesday so it would not interfere with Sunday, a religious day for many, or market day, which was often on Wednesday.

15

Election Day in the U.S.

The United States has a fixed Election Day. This means it falls on the same day every election year. To find the U.S. Election Day, look at the month of November on the calendar. Find the first Monday. Go to the Tuesday that follows it. That is Election Day!

- Election Day in the U.S. always falls on the Tuesday that follows the first Monday in November.

November   **2010**

SUNDAY	MONDAY	TUESDAY	WEDNESDAY	THURSDAY	FRIDAY	SATURDAY
	1	②	3	4	5	6
7	8	9	10	11	12	13
14	15	16	17	18	19	20
21	22	23	24	25	26	27
28	29	30				

DID YOU KNOW?

Many Americans speak Spanish. In Spanish, Election Day is called Elecciones.

Presidential Election Days are held on even-numbered years. Even-numbered years end in two, four, six, eight, or zero. Elections for other leaders are sometimes held on Election Day, too. They take place in a year with no presidential election.

Candidates in an election organize **campaigns** to try to get people to vote for them.

Public Holiday

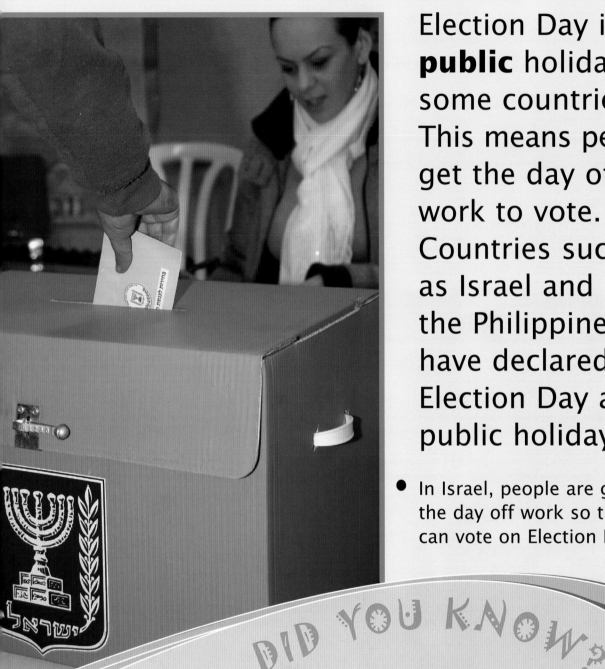

Election Day is a **public** holiday in some countries. This means people get the day off work to vote. Countries such as Israel and the Philippines have declared Election Day a public holiday.

- In Israel, people are given the day off work so they can vote on Election Day.

DID YOU KNOW?

Some United States leaders are trying to make a law that makes Election Day a public holiday in every state.

Some believe that more people will vote on Election Day if it is a public holiday.

In the United States, Election Day is a public holiday in some states, such as New York. Other states, such as California, have a law that lets people leave work early to vote.

- Some states make special laws for people to leave work early so they can vote.

19

Polling Stations

Most people vote at polling stations on Election Day. Polling stations are needed for just one day.

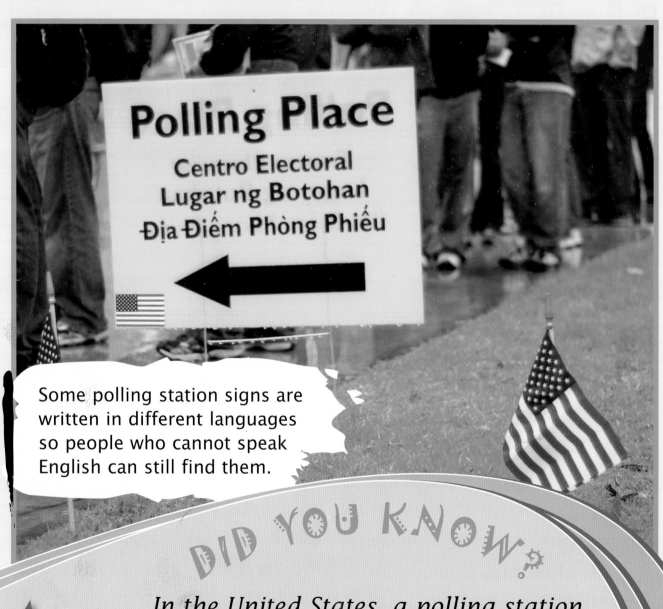

Polling Place
Centro Electoral
Lugar ng Botohan
Địa Điểm Phòng Phiếu

Some polling station signs are written in different languages so people who cannot speak English can still find them.

DID YOU KNOW?

In the United States, a polling station is often called a polling place.

They are set up in public places such as schools, offices, sports arenas, and church halls. Large cities have many polling stations.

Voters are told where they should vote before an election. People often vote at polling stations near their homes.

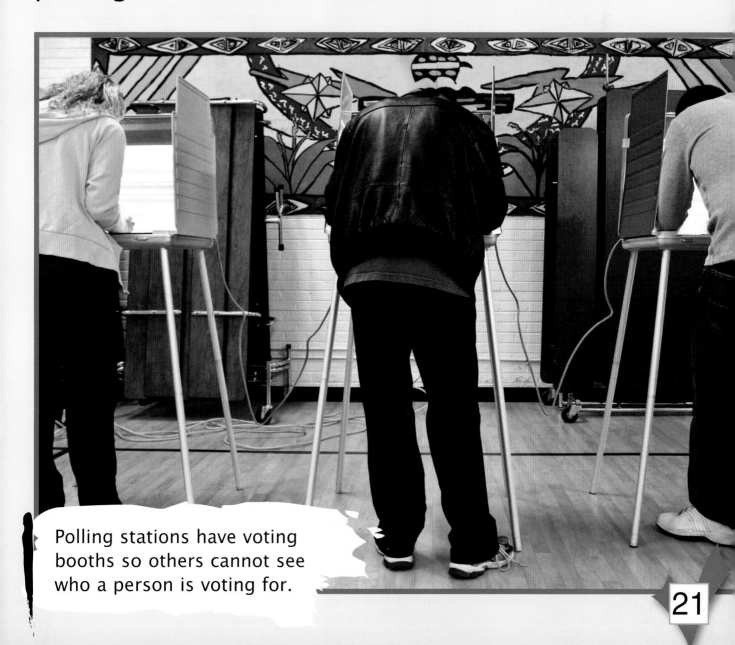

Polling stations have voting booths so others cannot see who a person is voting for.

21

Poll Workers

Poll workers are people who set up the polling stations, greet and help voters, and make sure everything is done correctly.

Poll workers help people at polling stations.

DID YOU KNOW?

*High school and college students can be poll workers, too. They ask their teachers for **permission** to help on Election Day.*

Poll watchers are people who watch to see that voting is done fairly. Returning officers help others vote. United States poll workers must be trained. They go to special classes, or read special books, on how to do this job. Many poll workers are volunteers, however, some are paid for their jobs.

- Poll workers often wear stickers or special clothing so that people know who they are.

23

How to Vote

A poll worker gives a voter one ballot. A ballot is a paper with names of possible leaders, or candidates.

Beside each candidate's name there is a place such as an empty circle or box to mark a choice. A voter marks one choice on the ballot.

After a person votes, he or she puts their ballot in the ballot box.

BALLOT

Some places use electronic voting systems. These systems have ballots displayed on a screen. The voter touches the screen or uses buttons to select the candidate they wish to vote for.

Poll workers help voters who do not know how to use the electronic voting systems.

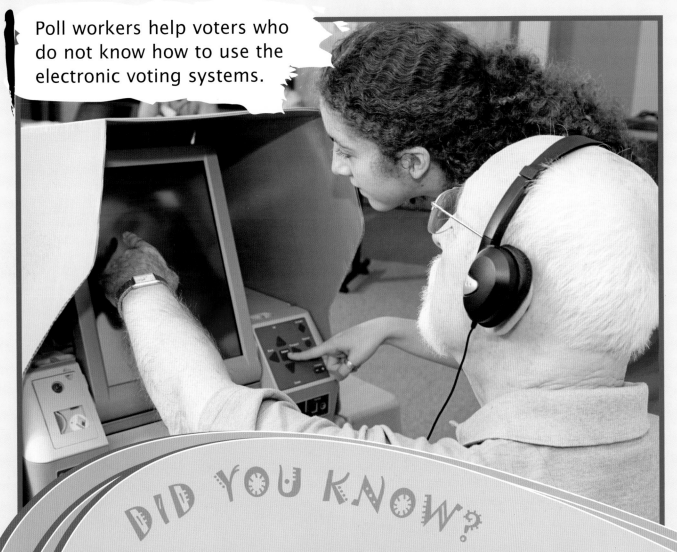

DID YOU KNOW?

Ballot boxes are sealed by a poll worker. The box is then taken to a place where the votes are counted. Police officers usually do this job.

And the Winner Is...

Votes can be counted by people or machines. People count votes and others watch them to see that it is done fairly. Sometimes two people will count each ballot to make sure they are correct.

Every vote is counted in an election.

When a machine is used, an officer sends the collected votes to a counting place. The leader with the majority of votes wins. A majority means the most votes.

In some places, ballots are put in a machine which counts the votes.

DID YOU KNOW?

Sometimes people use voting machines to vote. These ballots are read by machines, too.

27

Other Election Days

All democratic countries have Election Days. Some countries such as Britain do not have fixed Election Days. Their Election Day depends on when their leaders set it. Canada's leader can set the Election Day. However, it must be set at least by the third Monday in October every four years.

Canadians do not vote for the prime minister. Each citizen votes for someone in their own **community** who belongs to a **party**. The leader of the party with the most people elected becomes the prime minister.

In some countries, such as Australia, all citizens 18 years or older must vote. They pay a fine if they do not. Election Days are held on Saturdays when most people are not working.

All citizens of Australia who are 18 or older must vote on Election Day.

DID YOU KNOW?

Election Days in India are the largest in the world. Over 670 million citizens have the right to vote on this day!

29

Election Day Quiz

1. What happens on Election Day?
2. How old do you have to be to vote in most countries?
3. On which day of the week does Election Day fall in the United States?
4. What country holds Election Day on a Saturday?

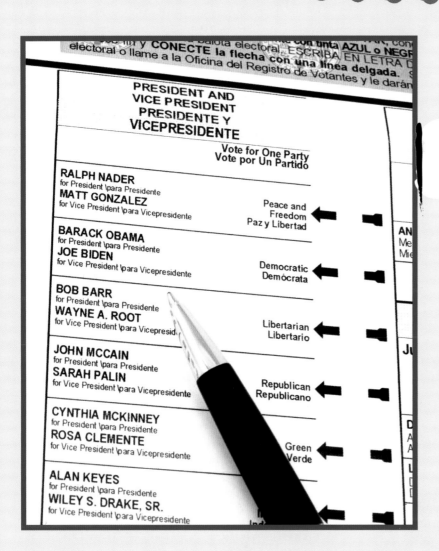

Every vote counts on Election Day!

5. Name a country that makes Election Day a public holiday.
6. What is a person who is trying to be elected as a leader called?

Answers: 1. Vote for a leader
2. 18
3. Tuesday
4. Australia
5. Israel or the Philippines
6. candidate

31

Glossary

absentee A person who is away

campaign An effort to get support from a group of people, often to obtain votes in an election

community A group of people living together in one area

democracy A type of government where everybody helps to pick a leader

dictator A ruler who forces leadership on a country

gender The quality of being male or female

government A group of people chosen by citizens to make laws

harvest Gathering of crops

medical Relating to health issues

military Soldiers that represent one country

monarch A ruler who is born into their position

party A group of people who agree on how laws should be made

permission To let someone do something

public A group of people who belong to a country

religious Relating to a person's belief in God

rights Freedom to do something

taxes Money paid to a government

vote To pick a leader

Index